Happy Birthday Peter

18th M...

Love

Rosemund

xx

Portrait of Father
Browne, taken in
1939 by his fellow-
Jesuit, Michael
Garahy.

Father Browne's DUBLIN

Photographs 1925-50

E.E. O'Donnell SJ

WOLFHOUND PRESS

'THE DAY BEFORE YESTERDAY: Fr Browne's Dublin'

An Exhibition at the Guinness Hopstore

During 1993, an exhibition of Father Frank Browne's Dublin photographs was presented by Peter Walsh, Curator of the Guinness Hopstore Exhibition Centre at St James' Gate, Dublin. This forms part of a series entitled 'A Dublin Album' based on important photographic collections which document the changing face of Dublin.

In his exhibition catalogue, Peter Walsh writes:

Fr Browne's pictures reflect what interested and attracted him. They represent the very personal, idiosyncratic and valid view of one Jesuit priest who was so much a part of his own time . . .

On 16th June 1927 a member of the Dublin Camera Club, William Harding, gathered a little group of 'doubting friends'(including Frank Browne) together in an upstairs room in Jury's Hotel, Dublin. Harding infused them with a large dose of his own infectious enthusiasm and perseverance and within a few weeks – with Harding as Director – the first ever Irish Salon of Photography was created and it went on to become the outstanding success of Dublin Civic Week 1927. Father Browne was one of the vice-presidents, under the presidency of Sir John Lavery . . .

Like all photographers, Fr Browne accumulated images that were not destined for the Salon or Gallery wall. And he had lots of other commitments and interests besides. He careered with exhilaration through periods of extraordinary upheaval. He was a fine teacher; photographed the *Titanic* and got off when she docked at Cobh; survived Ypres and the Somme; pleaded for Kevin Barry before his execution; became Superior of Gardiner Street Church; flew aeroplanes; preached missions and retreats; made ciné films of historic interest including one of the Eucharistic Congress in 1932 . . .

What then is the socio-political background to the Dublin photographs? The fledgling years of the Free State seem to have been a period characterised by an attempt to construct a specific national identity for Ireland, based exclusively on the shared historical experience of colonialism and on values which were thought to be essentially Irish – religious and nationalist fervour and a rigid moral stance. Insularity saw the new Ireland turning in on itself, nationalising particular beliefs and social mores. Catholicism represented not merely religious alignment but a predominant element in the struggle for economic and cultural independence from Britain ... there was huge unemployment and massive emigration and yet we managed to pretend that everything was wonderful. As Joseph Lee recently put it, we displayed 'self deception on an heroic scale'.

Frank Browne S.J. lived through all of this and his reflections of Dublin are multi-faceted. They show her great and mean streets, her rich and poor children, her politicians and priests, her trains and trams, her workers and her idlers, with equanimity. The emphases are on a city and its people as well as on the photographic art of the camera-wielder. His philosophy may well have proclaimed that, as summed up by Brooks Atkinson in 1951, 'the virtue of the camera is not the power it has to transform the photographer into an artist but the impulse it gives him to keep on looking.'

In his eulogy to his friend William Harding in 1929, Fr Browne expressed sentiments that might easily apply to himself:

'When other minds were set on the stern realities of political change, his could vision only a fellowship of art, in which all lovers of the camera would unite. It mattered not to him whether they were young or old – nay, truly, it mattered much to him that they should be both old and young – for in the vision he unfolded, the schoolboy with his 'Brownie' stood beside the veteran artist whose name had grown familiar to generations of photographers.'

Reprinted 1996
First published 1993 by
WOLFHOUND PRESS
68 Mountjoy Square
Dublin 1

© 1993 E.E. O'Donnell SJ

Photographs copyright © Francis Browne SJ
Collection

The publisher gratefully acknowledges the generous support of Guinness Ireland Ltd towards the publication of this volume.

British Library Cataloguing in Publication Data
Father Browne's Dublin
I. O'Donnell, E.E.
779.092

ISBN 0 86327 366 1

Profits made by the Jesuit Order from the sale of Father Browne's books and prints go to the Jesuit Solidarity Fund established to help counteract Ireland's serious unemployment problems both north and south of the border.

Book and cover design: Jan de Fouw. Cover photographs: 'Inspecting the Cameras at Kodak & Co, Grafton Street'(1930); back cover, 'Christ Church Cathedral from Cork Hill'(1940). Photographic prints by Davison & Associates, Dublin. Duotone separations by Typeform Repro. Typesetting by: Wolfhound Press. Printed in Hong Kong through World Print Ltd., 1996.

CONTENTS

continued overleaf

INTRODUCTION

Carmel Hannon at Sutton (1919). Father Browne's photographic career began in 1897, his first Dublin pictures being taken in 1906. Between that year and 1925 he was out of the country a lot. This sample photograph of his early work was developed just after his return from 'The Watch on the Rhine' with the Irish Guards.

Francis Mary Hegarty Browne was born in Cork, Ireland, in 1880. He belonged to a prominent family in that city, his grandfather (James Hegarty) holding the office of Lord Mayor and his uncle (Robert Browne) reigning as Bishop of the neighbouring See of Cloyne for nearly forty years.

Frank Browne went to school at the Bower Convent, Athlone, Christian Brothers College, Cork, Belvedere College, Dublin and Castleknock College in County Dublin. At the age of seventeen he went on a tour of Europe with his brother and his camera. His pictures of 1897, therefore, were the opening shots of a salvo of photography that is still reverberating nearly a hundred years later.

When he returned from the continent, he joined the Jesuits. His two years in the noviceship near Tullamore, County Offaly, were followed by a three-year classical course in the Royal University, Dublin. Then he studied philosophy for three years in Italy, near Turin. During the summer holidays he brought his camera to such places as Venice, Pompeii and Monte Carlo.

From 1906 to 1911, Frank Browne taught Latin and Greek at Belvedere College, Dublin, where he founded the Camera Club, the Cycling Club and the school magazine, all of which are still extant. During this time (in 1909) he sailed to Rome via Lisbon with his brother, his Uncle Robert and his camera. His sister, a nun in the papal household, was able to make arrangements for her family to have breakfast with the Pope. Afterwards, Frank took two photographs of His Holiness (now Saint) Pius X.

From 1912 to 1916, he studied theology in Milltown Park, Dublin. During these years the two greatest events of his life took place. In 1915 he was ordained a priest. But prior to that, in 1912 he sailed on the maiden voyage of R.M.V. *Titanic* from Southampton to Cherbourg and Queenstown (Cobh). His priceless album of Titanic photographs includes the last picture taken of Captain Edward Smith and the only picture ever taken in the liner's Marconi Room. After the iceberg had done its worst, Frank Browne's photographs appeared on the front pages of newspapers across the world.

Immediately following his theological studies, he was appointed Chaplain to the Irish Guards with whom he served on the Somme, at Ypres and at Passchendaele. Injured five times and gassed once, he won the Military Cross and Bar and the *Croix de Guerre*. His commanding officer, later Field Marshal Lord Alexander of Tunis, described Father Browne as 'the bravest man I ever met'.

During 1919 he remained with the Irish Guards during their

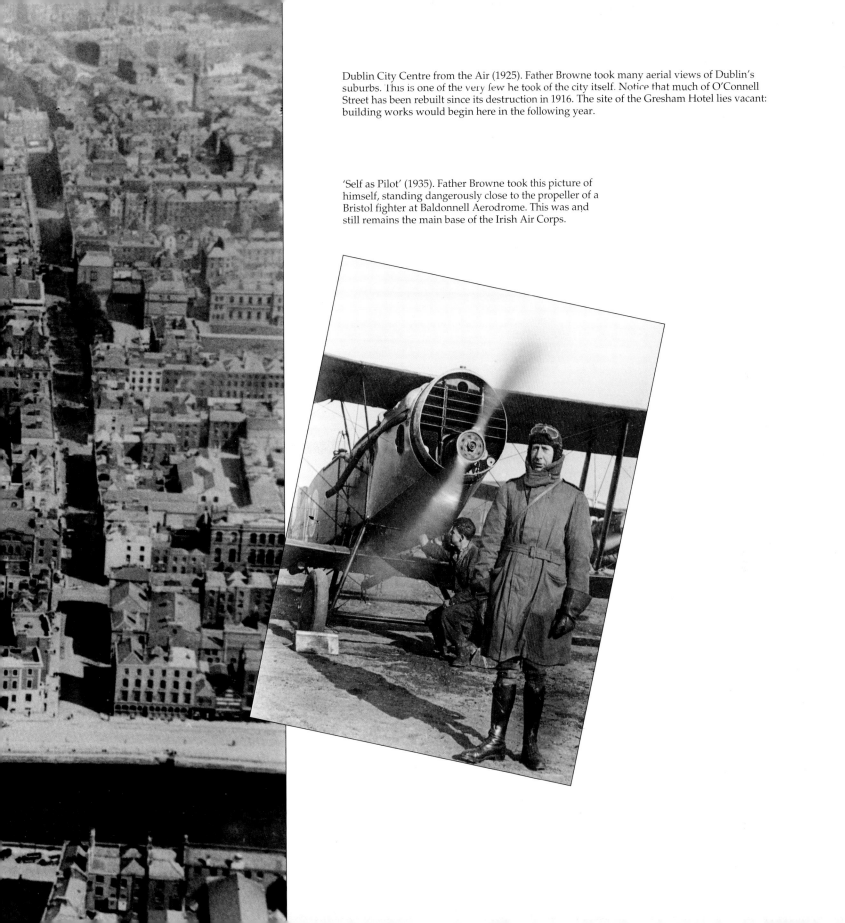

Dublin City Centre from the Air (1925). Father Browne took many aerial views of Dublin's suburbs. This is one of the very few he took of the city itself. Notice that much of O'Connell Street has been rebuilt since its destruction in 1916. The site of the Gresham Hotel lies vacant: building works would begin here in the following year.

'Self as Pilot' (1935). Father Browne took this picture of himself, standing dangerously close to the propeller of a Bristol fighter at Baldonnell Aerodrome. This was and still remains the main base of the Irish Air Corps.

'Watch on the Rhine'. The photographs he took during this time in Germany remain an important feature of his Collection.

In 1920 he returned to Dublin where he resumed his teaching career at Belvedere College and again taught photography to the boys in the Camera Club. He was appointed Superior of St Francis Xavier's Church, Gardiner Street, in 1922 but his health gradually deteriorated as a result of the World War I mustard gas. He was sent to Australia for two years to recuperate. He took hundreds of photographs in that continent as well as in South Africa, where he stopped on the voyage out, and in places like Ceylon, Aden, Suez, Salonika, Naples, Toulon, Gibraltar and Algeciras which he visited on the return journey.

Back in Dublin in 1926, he equipped himself with a new Contax camera and began to exhibit his work. Along with a group of like-minded enthusiasts (including William Harding, Editor of *The Camera*, Major R.H. Plews, President of the Photographic Society of Ireland, and Henry Dockrell, President of the Dublin Camera Club), he began to organise the biggest international photographic event ever held here. By all accounts the 'First Irish Salon of Photography' was the outstanding event of Dublin's Civic Week in 1927. Its President was Sir John Lavery, R.A. and its three vice-presidents were Hon. Mr Justice Hanna, K.C., General Eoin O'Duffy, Commissioner of the Garda Síochána and F.M. Browne S.J.

Such was the success of this venture that further 'Salons' were held every second year until the outbreak of World War II in 1939. Father Browne remained vice-president; he also exhibited some of his own work and won prizes for it. In 1931, for instance, he won four prizes: two of a guinea each and two of a half-guinea each. Other exhibitors in 1931 were Dr. John Williamson of Wales, Walter Orthaman of Australia and Alexander Keighley of England. For this information I am indebted to Mr Edward Chandler, the photographic historian.

For the remainder of his life, which would last another thirty years, Father Browne worked on the Retreats & Missions Staff of the Jesuit Order. This job brought him to parishes in all thirty-two counties of Ireland and to much of England, Scotland and Wales as well. Since his preaching work was mostly done in the evenings, he had plenty of time during the day for his photographic passion. By the time of his death he had accumulated a collection of 42,000 negatives, all neatly captioned and dated.

To put the photographs of this book into context, I should point out that Father Browne left very few positives behind him. Most of the negatives that I found in a trunk in the Jesuit archives in Dublin during 1985 were on a nitrate-based material that was rapidly deteriorating. Funds needed to transfer the Collection to safety-film were generously supplied by AIB Bank and its subsidiary Ark Life Assurance Company.

While the conservation work was in progress, the Collection was simultaneously indexed by computer. As a result of this operation, I am now able to say that nearly 35,000 of the Browne photographs were taken in Ireland and that, of these, just over 4,600 were taken in Dublin. The first Dublin pictures are dated 1906 – the year that Frank Browne founded the Camera Club in Belvedere. The last Dublin photographs were taken in 1958 at Gonzaga College, Sandford Road – where the Collection is now housed.

In 1987 Wolfhound Press illustrated my *Annals of Dublin* with over a hundred photographs from the Father Browne Collection. The pictures in this book received widespread acclaim in the media, not only in Ireland but in Great Britain and further afield.

The same publishers brought out *Father Browne's Ireland* in 1989, followed by *The Genius of Father Browne* in 1991. These two volumes included sixteen photographs of Dublin 'in the rare old times': these have not been duplicated in the present work. In this volume, *Father Browne's Dublin*, the presentation of the selection of photographs is chronological, beginning in 1925, when the photographer returned from Australia, and ending in 1950 as illness gradually forced him to forego photography as a serious pursuit.

Inevitably, this selection procedure necessitated the omission of many great photographs taken after World War II when both film and camera had improved enormously. On the other hand, the chronological method gives us a fascinating indication of the way Father Browne's work developed and affords a better insight into the way he viewed the capital over a period of decades.

To provide the interested reader with a brief context for these photographs, extracts from *The Annals of Dublin: Fair City* (Wolfhound Press 1987) are reproduced at the beginning of each decade. These have no specific relationship to the selection of photographs for each year; instead they provide a framework of reference to the major events that took place during the photographer's life.

To conclude, I want to thank Seamus Cashman of Wolfhound Press for his continuing (and well-placed) faith in Father Browne; and I must express my appreciation to Peter Walsh of Guinness Ireland Ltd. who inspired this volume with a splendid exhibition of Father Browne's Dublin photographs at the Guinness Hop store, St. James' Gate, Dublin.

E.E. O'Donnell S.J.
Gonzaga College
Dublin 6.

Dublin in the 1920s

Extracts from *The Annals of Dublin: Fair City*

1920 Government of Ireland Act provides for separate Parliaments for Northern Ireland and Southern Ireland.

Bloody Sunday: twelve spectators massacred by British forces during a football match at Croke Park in retaliation for IRA killings.

Kevin Barry, medical student, hanged in Mountjoy Jail for murder of soldier: first of twenty-four executions. (Fr Browne made a plea for Barry's life on the eve of his execution.)

IRA-man Sean Treacy and British Intelligence Officer Price kill one another in a shoot-out at Talbot Street.

1921 Custom House burnt down by IRA.

Second Dáil meets in the Oak Room of the Mansion House. It is an illegal body until the Anglo-Irish Treaty is signed on 6th December. 26 of the 32 counties of Ireland become the Irish Free State.

Kingstown is renamed Dún Laoghaire, its original name.

1922 Dáil Eireann approves the Treaty with Britain by a majority of seven after protracted discussion. Provisional Government of the Irish Free State constituted, with Arthur Griffith elected President of Dáil Eireann. British forces and officials leave Dublin.

Liam O'Flaherty, writer, with a handful of unemployed dockers, seizes the Rotunda in January and raises a red flag. This token 'Irish Soviet Republic' fell in three days without a shot being fired. O'Flaherty's Dublin thrillers will include *The Assassin*, based on the assassination of Kevin O'Higgins in 1927.

Death of Arthur Griffith.

First meeting of newly-elected Dáil in Leinster House: William T. Cosgrave becomes first Taoiseach. Michael Collins comes to prominence as a minister. Later assassinated in County Cork.

Timothy Healy appointed first Governor-General of Irish Free State.

Civil War begins (to last till 1923) between the supporters and the opponents of the Treaty. Four Courts bombarded and mined: Ireland's official Public Records go up in smoke.

Publication (in Paris) of James Joyce's Dublin saga, *Ulysses*.

1923 Civil War ends.

Cumann na nGaedhael political party founded by William Cosgrave who supports Anglo-Irish Treaty of 1921 and forms a government which will remain in office until 1932.

Cenotaph in honour of Arthur Griffith and Michael Collins is unveiled outside Leinster House.

Garda Síochána established (see 1925 below).

Irish Free State joins League of Nations.

W B Yeats wins Nobel Prize for Literature.

Members of the Legion of Mary begin rehabilitation work among Dublin's prostitutes (The Legion was founded by Frank Duff, a Dubliner, in 1921).

Brendan Behan born at 14 Russell Street.

1924 Ceremonial inauguration of the first Chief Justice of the Irish Free State in Dublin Castle. The Irish language is used in court for the first time in centuries.

Release of 15,000 Civil War prisoners in Dublin and countrywide.

1925 G. B. Shaw is awarded the Nobel Prize for Literature.

Royal Dublin Society moves from Leinster House to Ballsbridge.

Dublin Metropolitan Police amalgamated with the Garda Síochána .

1926 Radio Station 2RN begins broadcasting.

Fianna Fáil party formed by Eamon de Valera from old Sinn Féin: it refuses to take the 'Treaty Oath' or to sit in Dáil Eireann.

Bewley's Café opens in Grafton Street. Joshua Bewley, an Englishman, opened his first café in Sycamore Alley in 1846. He soon moved to South Great George's Street. In 1916, a second branch was opened in Westmoreland Street.

'Disturbances' at The Abbey Theatre during Sean O'Casey's play, *The Plough and the Stars*. W B Yeats tells the audience: 'You have disgraced yourselves again!'

1927 Fianna Fáil deputies take 'Treaty oath' and enter Dáil Eireann.

Kevin O'Higgins, Minister for Justice, is assassinated.

James MacNeill appointed Governor-General on retirement of Timothy Healy.

1928 Irish Free State issues its first coins and currency-notes.

Lord Longford opens Gate Theatre. Hilton Edwards and Mícheál MacLiammóir find a stage.

W B Yeats writes to Sean O'Casey on behalf of Abbey Theatre rejecting *The Silver Tassie*. O'Casey, like many another Dublin writer will remain in London in voluntary exile.

1929 GPO re-opens for first time since 1916.

Centenary of Catholic Emancipation: 400,000 people attend Mass in Phoenix Park.

William Smith O'Brien's statue is moved to O'Connell Street (from D'Olier Street); statue of William of Orange removed from College Green – by nationalists' gun powder!

Children of Finglas (1925). When this photograph was taken,
Finglas was quite a small village on the outskirts of Dublin.
The children shown here are taking a Sunday afternoon rest
near the River Tolka, not far from King William's Ramparts.

'Where my Caravan hath
Rested': Saggart, County
Dublin (1925). Ireland's
'Travelling People' are said
to have originated near
here at Tallaght.

Killiney Strand (1925). A popular watering-place for Dubliners
ever since the opening of the Dublin and South Eastern Railway
in 1859. Donkey-rides on the sands were an enjoyable feature
of Killiney right up to the early 1960s.

Sand-dredgers at Lucan (1925). The dredgers lived in a part of Lucan quaintly known as 'Hell'. Sand from the bed of the River Liffey was exported from Lucan to all parts of the capital as well as to builders further afield.

'Census Day', Tallaght (1926). The first census of the population of the twenty-six counties was taken by the Free State Government on 24 May, 1926. This old man, rather bewildered by all the questions, asked Fr Browne, 'What am I to do with the paper?'

'The Caretaker' on the South Bull Wall (1926). The boots probably belong to swimmers who have gone for a dip at the Half Moon Club further along the Bull Wall near Poolbeg Lighthouse.

16

Mr. Tim Healy with Fr J. O'Reilly at a Garden Party in Raheny (1926). Parnell's erstwhile associate and ultimate rival in the Irish Party at Westminster, Tim Healy became the first Governor General of the Irish Free state in 1922.

Sunday Morning in the Snow, Gardiner Street (1927).

Dispatching the Mail for the Kish Lightship (1927).

Watching the Trains at Kingsbridge (1928). The Four Courts Hotel no longer exists. The boy is perched on the wall of the Great Southern Railway goods-yard, watching shunting in progress.

Window-shopping on Grafton Street (1927). This is about as near as these lads could get to the goods on display. Presumably they come from the nearby Aungier Street area and have been sent out to collect the morning milk.

'Through the Windscreen' (1928). Taken while driving down alongside the Grand Canal at Portobello.

'Simple Pleasures', Hardwicke Street (1929). The tenements in this street which was once among the most fashionable in the metropolis   were demolished in 1954 to make way for new Corporation flats.

Commercial Buildings, Dame Street (1929). In 1978 the disproportionate Central Bank replaced the buildings of the Dublin Chamber of Commerce which itself had replaced the Ouzel Galley Society in 1783.

Young Rugby Fans at Donnybrook (1930). Watching the Belvedere v. Blackrock College Senior Cup Match. Now there is a stand on the right. In 1930 this ground was the property of Bective Rangers. More recently it was acquired by the Leinster Branch of the Irish Rugby Football Union.

Dublin in the 1930s

Extracts from *The Annals of Dublin: Fair City*

1930 Borough of Dún Laoghaire established.

Censorship Board appointed: in due course, it will ban most modern classics in the English language.

Dublin's urban area extended to include Pembroke and Rathmines.

H V Morton, the English travel-writer, visits the Dublin Zoo and is fascinated by a preserved elephant's foot bearing the inscription; 'Sita, who killed her keeper and was shot, 11th June, 1903.'

1931 River Dodder bursts its banks: damage estimated at £40,000.

First issue of *The Irish Press*.

Death of Harry Clarke, stained-glass designer.

Irish Academy of Letters founded by Yeats and Shaw in Dublin. Its first members are: Austin Clarke, Padraic Colum, St John Ervine, Oliver Gogarty, Frederick Robert Higgins, Brinsley MacNamara, George Moore, T C Murray, Frank O'Connor, Peadar O'Donnell, Sean O'Faolain, Liam O'Flaherty, Seumas O'Sullivan, Forrest Reid, Lennox Robinson, George W Russell (AE), G B Shaw, Miss E OE Somerville, James Stephens, Francis Stuart and W B Yeats. Sean O'Casey refuses (violently) to join; James Joyce also refuses.

Bi-centenary celebrations of Royal Dublin Society.

1932 Eucharistic Congress: massive crowds celebrate in Phoenix Park and on O'Connell Bridge.

Army Comrades Association founded (see 1933).

General Election: Fianna Fáil win. Eamon de Valera becomes Taoiseach (for next sixteen years). Domhnall O Buachalla sworn in as Governor-General – briefed to make a nonsense of the Office.

1933 General E O'Duffy is elected leader of Army Comrades Association, now known as the National Guard (The Blueshirts). The Association is soon banned. Under a new name, the Young Ireland Association, it will be banned again the following year. Fascist-type demonstrations are held at the Mansion House and around the country. O'Duffy will lead 700 volunteers to fight for Franco in the Spanish Civil War in 1936.

Municipal Gallery opens in remodelled Charlemont House on Parnell Square, with a room left empty for Hugh Lane's donation of paintings which have been (controversially) kept by the National Gallery in London. Up to this time, the gallery was in Clonmel House, Harcourt Street.

United Irish Party (later to be called Fine Gael) is launched under presidency of Eóin O'Duffy.

1934 Statue of Cú Chulainn (Sheppard) unveiled in GPO.

Eóin O'Duffy resigns from the Fine Gael party.

No Dublin newspapers from July to October due to a trade dispute.

1935 Transport strike in Dublin lasts from March to May.

Sale or importation of contraceptives forbidden.

Death of the writer and painter, George Russell (AE).

1936 Aer Lingus: inaugural flight from Dublin to Bristol under the name of Irish Sea Airways. Dublin Airport (see 1940) has yet to be built, so the flight leaves from Baldonnel airfield.

Ireland's first seismograph built at Rathfarnham Castle: it will earn an international reputation for its accuracy in measuring earthquakes. Now in Maynooth College Museum.

Liffey Reservoir Act empowers ESB to carry out hydro-electric scheme at Poulaphuca.

1937 New Constitution. Irish Free State becomes 'Eire'.

General Election: Fianna Fáil win again.

1938 Anglo-Irish Agreement signed in London. 'Treaty Ports' returned by Great Britain. *The Irish Times* comments: 'No British Government would survive for twenty-four hours if it should attempt to bring undue pressure to bear on Belfast ... Only by the promotion of more intimate relations between Dublin and London can the suspicions of Northern Ireland be allayed; but the process will take time.'

Hospitals Trust formed as statutory body. First sweepstake had been held in 1930. Will close in 1987 on the arrival of the National Lottery.

Douglas Hyde, a Protestant, is elected first President. Vice-regal Lodge becomes Áras an Uachtaráin, the presidential residence.

First meeting of new Irish Senate, Seanad Eireann. (It was of the old Senate – 1922 – of the Irish Free State that Edward MacLysaght, Gogarty and W B Yeats were members; this was abolished in 1936).

Another General Election won by Fianna Fáil.

Eamon de Valera is elected president of assembly of League of Nations.

1939 World War II starts. Ireland neutral. Petrol rationed.

W B Yeats dies at Rocquebrune, France.

Magazine Fort (Phoenix Park) raided by the IRA at Christmas: over a million rounds of ammunition stolen.

Publication (in Paris) of James Joyce's *Finnegans Wake*.

Inspecting the Cameras
at Kodak & Co.,
Grafton Street (1930).
The Kodak
headquarters in Dublin
was on Rathmines
Road but, until
recently, there was a
retail outlet on Grafton
Street where Father
Browne was a frequent
and popular visitor.

Fallen Horse, O'Connell Bridge (1930). When horse-drawn traffic was at its height, this was a frequent and unfortunate sight on the city streets. When wet or icy, cobblestones were a nightmare for horses, donkeys and cyclists.

Taxi Rank, taken from the roof of the Shelbourne Hotel (1930). Father Browne took at least twenty of his Dublin photographs with the camera pointing vertically downwards. The unusual perspective gives interest to the commonplace.

The Empty Pond, St. Stephen's Green (1931). 'The Green' is the largest city square in Europe. Up to 1880 it was the preserve of the local residents. Then Lord Ardilaun of Guinness's Brewery laid it out as a park, built this pond and opened the gates to the public.

Newsboy at Harcourt Street Station (1930). Wilkinson's terminal building for the Dublin and South Eastern Railway was built in 1859. The station, along with the railway line, was closed in 1959 to the dismay of southside commuters.

'Yo-yo Girls' (1931). Taken on Cavendish Row near the Parnell Monument at the top of O'Connell Street.

''Shadow of Parliament' (1931). The shadow on Trinity College is being cast by the Bank of Ireland which was where the Irish parliament sat until the Act of Union of 1800. The building was designed by Edward Lovett Pearce in 1729 but the shadow actually comes from the extension added by James Gandon in 1785.

32

'Affixing a Plaque', O'Connell Street (1931). Outside the Hibernian Bank, the plaque was commemorating the fifteenth anniversary of the Easter Rising of 1916.

'Modern Art' (1931). A shot from the train window on the Loop Line at Talbot Street. In the background, one can make out advertisements for Beatty's curtains and for Kingston's shirts which 'made all the difference'.

Children's Mass in the Phoenix Park during the Eucharistic Congress (1932). This Mass was celebrated on Saturday, 25 June. Tens of thousands of children from all over Ireland were present: a scene comparable to the one in Galway during the 1979 Papal visit.

O'Connell Street during the Eucharistic Congress (1932). Taken at 3.00 p.m. on Sunday, 26 June, from the roof of Kennedy & McSharry's menswear shop on Westmoreland Street. Subsequent pictures show O'Connell Street filling up.

Congress Crowds, Lower Gardiner Street (1932). Near the junction of Talbot Street we can see that the inner city was decorated lavishly. These people are waiting for a glimpse of Cardinal Glennon of St. Louis who was going to preach in Gardiner Street Church.

O'Connell Street during the Eucharistic Congress (1932). After Mass in the Phoenix Park, the crowds converged on O'Connell Bridge where Solemn Benediction was given by the Papal Legate, Cardinal Lauri. Perched on a Westmoreland Street rooftop, Father Browne made a motion-picture of the event. He took this photograph at 5.30 p.m.

Distinguished Guests at the Eucharistic Congress (1932). During High Mass in the Phoenix Park on Sunday, 26 June a special section was reserved for people like G.K. Chesterton and Count John McCormack who can be identified here by their portly build: the former in lay clothes, the latter in the uniform of a Papal Count.

'The Face at the Window',
Harcourt Street Station
(1933).

The Custom House and
Eden Quay, viewed from
the top deck of a Tram on
O'Connell Bridge (1933).

Burst Water-main, Summerhill (1933). This particular main was
laid in 1868, the year that Vartry Water came to Dublin from the
new reservoir at Roundwood.

The Gasometer on Sir John Rogerson's Quay (1933). Gas-light
was installed along Dublin's city streets in 1825. As domestic
demand grew, so did the size of the gas-holders. Father Browne
photographed this monster from every angle and took several
panoramic views of the city from its dizzy height.

Reflections on a Canal (1933). This is the Royal Canal lock at the North Strand. The lock-keeper's cottage remains intact. In the background is Newcomen Bridge, built in 1790 and named after the banker who was also a director of the Canal Board.

A Sleety Day on the Halfpenny Bridge (1933). So called from the original toll exacted, this, the only foot-bridge across the Liffey, was built in 1816 and named after the Dublin-born general who had defeated Napoleon at Waterloo in the previous year.

'Emergency Services' in O'Connell Street (1935). The busmen were on strike from March until May and Army lorries were called into action. The Garda in the foreground wears a helmet reminiscent of the Dublin Metropolitan Police who had been amalgamated with the Garda Síochána (established 1923) in 1925.

Barge on the Grand Canal at Leeson Street Bridge (1935). When this canal opened in 1759, its Dublin terminus was beside the Guinness Brewery at St. James' Gate. The extension to the Liffey, including the stretch shown here, was not constructed until 1790.

Book-stall at Dun Laoghaire (1934). Located beside the East Pier of the harbour.

'A Helping Hand', Booterstown (1936). Mrs Helen White and her daughter, Margaret, were friends of the photographer.

'The 'Outside Beds' at Cappagh Hospital (1936).

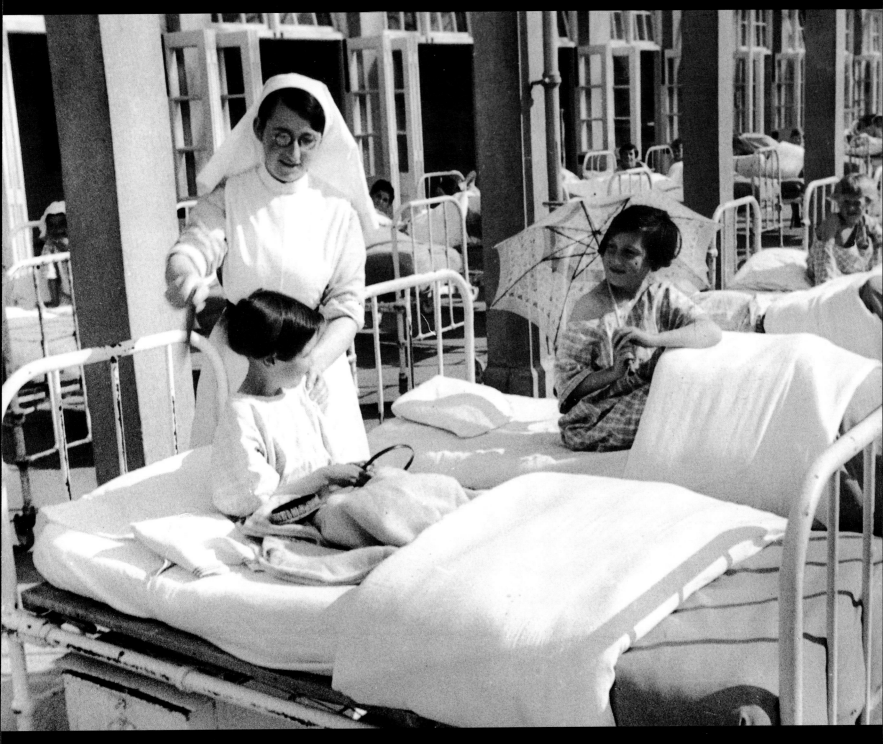

First Holy Communion at Cappagh Hospital (1937). A poignant reminder of the ravages of tuberculosis before modern medicine brought that disease under control. On this occasion, gifts were sent to the children by Colonel McCalmont of Mount Juliet who had served in the Irish Guards with Fr Browne during World War I.

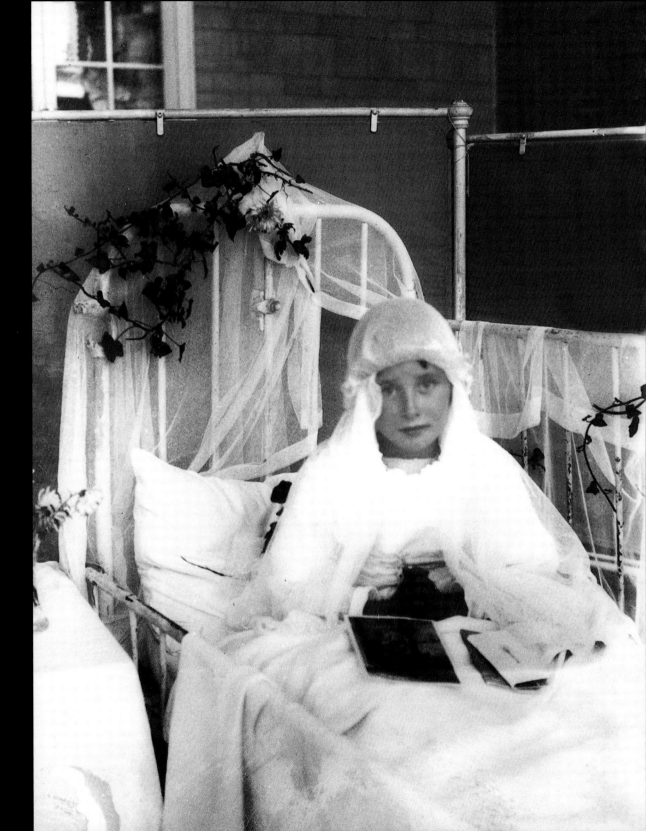

Passengers on the Mail Boat (1937). These photographs were taken on the s.s. *Scotia.* Father Browne loved to travel by ship. Immediately introducing himself to the Captain, he would be allowed on to the bridge and would photograph every aspect of the crew's work from departure to arrival. The *Scotia* was a sister ship of another mail boat, s.s. *Hibernia.*

Greaser at Work, Inchicore (1938). Taken at the engineering workshops of the Great Southern Railway. Sancton Wood designed the nearby Kingsbridge terminus for the Great Southern & Western Railway in 1845. The G.S.R. and the Dublin United Tramway Company were taken over by C.I.E. in 1944.

Gardiner Street Fire (1938). The Dublin Fire Brigade in action. Established in 1862, the Brigade has ever been a source of pride for Dublin's citizens. Perhaps its proudest moment was in 1941 when the Dublin Fire Brigade rushed to Belfast to help that city in the aftermath of severe bombing.

Make-up for the Opera, Belvedere College (1938). An annual production of a Gilbert and Sullivan opera took place during the Christmas holidays at Father Browne's *alma mater*. This year it was the turn of *Patience*, the skit on Oscar Wilde.

'Winners at the Feis' (1938). Misses Marie Jones and Carmel Kiernan on the piano at 7 Ailesbury Road. The Feis Ceoil, based in Molesworth Street, gives awards for music and singing. James Joyce won its bronze medal in 1904.

Sentry at Dublin
Castle (1938).

The Crampton Memorial, Pearse Street (1938). Erected
in honour of the Surgeon-General of His Majesty's
Forces in 1862, this strange work featured in Cosgrave's
Illustrated History of Dublin with this caustic comment:
'The sculptor [J. Kirk] hopes it will be a monument to
himself as well as to Sir Philip Crampton'.

The Maids at Linden (1939). These smiling girls were on the
domestic staff of Linden Convalescent Home, Blackrock. Father
Browne was a patient there at the time.

Off-loading at Dublin Port (1938).
At Sir John Rogerson's Quay.

'Farewell to Dublin' (1939). Taken aboard the B&I
Liverpool ferry, m.v. Munster, on leaving the North
Wall. The gasworks can be seen in the background.

'Evening Shadows',
St. Stephen's Green (1939).

'From Bombs to Bonnives' (1939).
Europe is on the brink of World
War II but Irish piglets still need
to be fed. The 'Russian Bombshell'
refers to the Nazi-Soviet pact
signed by Ribbentrop and
Molotov on 29 September.

(Below) St. Audeon's Church, Cornmarket (1939). This was the first church built by the Normans a year after their capture of Dublin in 1170. It stands on the site of an early Celtic building dedicated to St. Colum Cille. The tower contains Dublin's oldest bells which used to be rung during stormy weather to remind the citizens to pray for those at sea.

(Above) Findlater's Church, Parnell Square (1939). Taken from the roof of Belvedere College on Great Denmark Street. The Abbey Presbyterian Church was designed by Heaton in 1864 and financed by the well-known grocer, Alexander Findlater, whose main outlet was on Upper O'Connell Street with branches throughout the city and suburbs.

Cricket at Linden (1939). An imaginative wicket
at Linden Convalescent Home, Blackrock.

'The Ice-cream Man', Stillorgan (1939). Tricycled ice-cream men were a magnet for youngsters and were often seen parked outside National Schools.

This portrait of an accordionist was taken on Hawkins Street, outside the Regal Rooms Cinema. This small cinema was part of the Theatre Royal which had been burned down in 1895 but re-opened as Dublin's largest theatre two years later. It was demolished to make way for 'Hawkins House' office-block in 1962.

Dublin in the 1940s

Extracts from *The Annals of Dublin: Fair City*

First issue of *The Bell* magazine, edited by Sean O'Faolain. It will last until 1954.

Institute for Advanced Studies founded.

Dublin Airport (D FitzGerald) opens.

John Charles McQuaid becomes Catholic Archbishop of Dublin, a post he will hold until his retirement in 1972.

Poulaphuca Reservoir built. By 1987, it will supply 24,000,000 gallons of water to Dublin every day. For Poulaphuca Power Station, see 1943.

Corpus Christi Church (J Robinson) opens in Whitehall.

1941   Dublin Fire Brigade rushes to Belfast to help in aftermath of bombing. *The Daily Telegraph* reports:

A wave of gratitude for Eire's errand of mercy has swept the city (of Belfast) overnight, establishing a bond of sympathy between North and South Ireland which no British or Irish statesman has been able to establish in a generation.

German bombs fall in Terenure and Harold's Cross in January: no casualties. In May, however, the North Strand is bombed with 37 people killed and 90 injured. After the War, West Germany will pay over £327,000 compensation.

Molyneux Asylum closes.

Dublin Grand Opera Society founded. It succeeds the Dublin Operatic Society which had been founded in 1928 by Signor Viani. First production: *Il Trovatore*, at the Gaiety Theatre.

James Joyce dies in Zurich.

1942   Food rationing intensified.

Petrol shortage keeps Dublin cars off the streets till end of War. Due to fuel shortage, Dublin trams have to stop running at 9.30 pm.

Federated Union of Employers is certified as a trade union.

Howth Urban District is absorbed into County Dublin.

Central Bank established as currency authority.

1943   Electricity: the Liffey scheme begins to come on stream for the ESB with four megawatts coming from Golden Falls. In the following year, Poulaphuca will generate 15mw and in 1947 a further 15mw. The scheme will be completed in 1949 with the 4mw power-station at Leixlip.

General Election: Fianna Fáil retain power.

1944   General Election: Fianna Fáil retain power again.

Córas Iompair Eireann established. It takes over the Great Southern Railways Company and the Dublin United Tramway Company and is 'to generally control and reorganize transport'.

1945   World War II ends. Dublin Government attacked by Churchill in victory speech. Eamon de Valera responds in memorable statement which may be read in full in *The Irish Press*, 17th May, 1945.

John McCormack, the operatic and concerto singer, dies and is buried at Deansgrange.

Seán T O'Kelly elected President.

1946   Thousands of Dubliners volunteer to save the precarious harvest.

Clann na Poblachta, left-wing party, founded by Seán MacBride.

Teachers' strike leaves 40,000 pupils out of primary school from 20th March to 31st October.

1947   Eamon de Valera signs Marshall Aid-to-Europe plan on behalf of Eire.

Bread rationed in Dublin.

Celtic Congress meets in Dublin with overseas delegations from Brittany, Cornwall, the Isle of Man, Scotland and Wales.

1948   General Election: John A Costello takes over from Eamon de Valera as Taoiseach. Coalition Government.

Foundation of An Taisce, the National Trust for Ireland. Headquarters now at Tailor's Hall.

Statue of Queen Victoria is removed from the fore-court of Leinster House.

Death of Dr Paschal Robinson, Eire's first Papal Nuncio.

1949   Republic of Ireland established.

College of Industrial Relations holds its first classes in 35 Lower Leeson Street under the name of the Catholic Worker's College. It will move to its present location in Ranelagh in 1951.

The last Dublin tram runs from Nelson Pillar to Dalkey on 10th July.

First issue of *The Sunday Press*.

'Children's Tea-party', Temple Street (1940). Taken at the front steps
of one of the tenements that were demolished in 1954. Originally,
this Georgian building would have been one of the finest in the city.
Temple Street was part of the Gardiner Estate, developed in the
middle years of the eighteenth century by Luke Gardiner.

Christ Church Cathedral from Cork Hill (1940). Looking up Lord Edward Street, we have the Evening Mail offices on the right and the Corporation Rates Office on the left. The latter was designed by Thomas Ivory as Newcomen's Bank in 1781. Cork Hill is named after Hugh Boyle, Earl of Cork.

Gas-driven Lorry (1941). The 'Eclipse' model of the improved gas motor can be seen attached to the running-board of the lorry. Petrol was not rationed: it was simply not available so private cars had to be laid up for the duration of 'the emergency'.

A Portrait of Malachi Horan, Ballinascorney (1942). Mr. Horan was ninety-three years of age when this photograph was taken. The remarkable memoirs of his life in the Dublin Mountains were recorded by Dr. George Little, President of the Old Dublin Society and published as *Malachi Horan Remembers*.

(Above) O'Connell Street from Elvery's (1942). Pedestrians and a hand-cart.

(Left) O'Connell Street from Elvery's (1942). Elvery's sports-goods emporium which later moved to Abbey Street stood at the corner of O'Connell Street that was later acquired by the Evening Press. It was known as 'Jumbo House' from the effigy of an elephant which stood outside a first-floor window.

Suspended scaffolding, Kildare Street (1942). This was the first use in Ireland of suspended scaffolding.

The Breadman on Parnell Street (1942). The horse-drawn breadvans of Rourke's Bakery continued to ply the streets long after the war. Near the junction of Marlborough Street we see a petrol-driven lorry delivering kegs of beer: essential supplies had to get through.

1943

The Central Catholic Library (1943). Located at 74 Merrion Square, this establishment was opened in 1922 in Westmoreland Street. It moved to Hawkins Street before acquiring the premises shown here. The founder, Father Stephen Browne S.J. was a contemporary of the photographer. They were not relatives.

Playing at the Fountain, St. Stephen's Green (1943). The boys
are preparing to race their boats, made from half-opened,
empty sardine-tins with the opened pieces acting as sails. Small
fortunes were won and lost at this pastime.

Mrs Stevens , with Marjorie and daughter, Lucan (1943).

'Cleanliness next to Godliness' (1945). Eliza Fanning at work in the sanctuary of St. Francis Xavier's Church Gardiner Street, where the photographer had been Superior from 1922 to 1928.

St. Stephen's Green in the Fog (1944). At the top of Grafton
Street stands the Memorial Arch, completed in 1907, in honour
of the Dublin soldiers who fell in the Boer War. It was known to
Nationalist citizens as 'Traitors Gate'.

The Last of the Tenements, Sean McDermott Street (1944).
When these houses were built, the thoroughfare was named
Gloucester Street; before that, it was called Great Martin's Lane.
Seán Mac Diarmada, one of the signatories of the Proclamation
of Independence, was executed in 1916.

Signalman A. Cooney at work in the signal cabin at Balbriggan
Railway Station (1946). The photographer noted that the
Bundoran Express had just passed through – a service
discontinued with the closing of the Bundoran line in 1957.

Loading the Country Bus, Aston's Quay (1947). Before Busáras was opened in 1953, the provincial buses had their terminus here. It is the Kilkenny bus that is being loaded; the three C.I.E. porters in the foreground are awaiting an arrival from Granard, Co. Longford.

Georgian Mews, Leeson Court (1946). This was taken from a rear window of 35 Lower Leeson Street. To-day the row of 'stables' is changed beyond recognition. In the background is the Royal Victoria Eye & Ear Hospital which was built in 1897.

Howth Castle and Ireland's Eye (1947). The first (and last) sentence of *Finnegans Wake* ends with the words, 'Howth Castle and Environs'. Joyce immortalised the home of Sir Almeric Tristram St. Lawrence, the Norman knight who built the first castle here in 1177.

The Lutyens Loggia at Howth Castle (1947). The last decade of the nineteenth century Commander Gaisfort St. Lawrence commissioned Sir Edwin Lutyens to design the west tower of the castle. Sir Edwin also designed this beautiful loggia which connects the Sidney Hall with the lawn.

Larkhill Church, Whitehall (1948). Taken during the Women's Mission which was so well attended that seating had to be provided in the centre aisle. The preacher in the pulpit, top left, is Father Robert Louis Stevenson S.J.

Dolphin's Barn during the Black Winter of 1947. Taken on the South Circular Road. Father Browne was giving a Mission in this parish during the week of 7 March.

'Sand Art', Balbriggan (1948).

Twin tubs in the wash-room at Manresa House (1948). Baymount Castle (built 1838) was part of the Vernon Estate and belonged to the Ardilaun branch of the Guinness family before becoming a girls' boarding school. This picture was taken during renovations after the Jesuits acquired the building for use as a Retreat House.

Bus Queue, Upper O'Connell Street (1948).
The Carlton Cinema can be seen on the left.

Áras an Uachtaráin (1948). This is the South Front of the house, taken from the east. Before becoming the presidential residence, it was built as the home of the Phoenix Park Ranger in 1751 and enlarged in 1782 when it became the Vice- Regal Lodge.

Crooksling Sanatorium (1949). This was taken on the women's verandah of the sanatorium in the foothills of the Dublin Mountains.

1949

Milltown Park after the Fire (1949). One Jesuit, Fr Jim Johnson aged
33, died and several others were seriously injured in a fire at the
theologate on 10 February. Fr Browne was ordained here in 1915.

Dublin in the 1950s

Extracts from *The Annals of Dublin: Fair City*

[Although this volume does not include Fr Browne's 1950s Dublin pictures, apart from the closing image on page 96, the extracts from *The Annals of Dublin: Fair City* for the decade are useful in providing a context for the changes that were now about to take place in Dublin and throughout Ireland. An industrial and business 'revolution' is set to begin; the country will open up to the world outside, and show signs of challenging its own, often cosy, perceptions of itself. The Irish Free State is heading towards a more mature Republic of Ireland. But tradition is not discarded, nor is it easily changed. The second half of the twentieth century will bring rapid and often uncontrolled change to the Dublin portrayed in these photographs.]

1950   George Bernard Shaw, Dublin playwright, dies in England.

Gonzaga College founded by Jesuit Order in former home of the Bewley family, Ranelagh.

Industrial Development Authority established.

Banks closed from December 6th (for 2 months) owing to a strike of their officials.

1951   Archbishop of Dublin, John Charles McQuaid, and other Catholic bishops object to government's Mother and Child Scheme by which free medical care would be given to mothers and their children up to sixteen years of age. The Minister for Health, Dr Noel Browne (who had organised the fight against tuberculosis since 1948), resigns, Government falls.

General Election won by Fianna Fáil: Eamon de Valera returns as Taoiseach.

Professor E T S Walton of Trinity College Dublin shares Nobel Prize for Physics. (He had worked on the transmutation of atomic nuclei).

Abbey Theatre burnt down. It will reopen in 1966.

1952   No Dublin newspapers for six weeks due to dispute in printing trade.

Inaugural meeting of Irish Management Institute.

Bord Fáilte established to promote tourism.

1953   Chester Beatty Library opens. Priceless collection of oriental art treasures donated to the State by the American oil magnate, Sir Alfred Chester Beatty, Ireland's first honorary citizen.

Busárus (Michael Scott) opens. Dublin's first modern office-block and Central Bus Station is derided as 'The Glass House'.

An Tóstal: Community Festival. The flower-bed on O'Connell Bridge with its Bowl of Light is nick-named 'The Tomb of the Unknown Gurrier'.

1954   General Election: John A Costello again becomes Taoiseach of Coalition Government.

Evening Press launched.

Tolka Bridge collapses due to flood: the fallen bridge acts as a dam and causes even more flooding. Local residents have to be rescued by rowing-boat. Until a Bailey bridge is erected, the Belfast trains have their terminus at the tiny Clontarf station.

1955   Ireland joins the United Nations.

First performance (in London) of Samuel Beckett's *Waiting for Godot*.

1956   Death of Alfie Byrne who was ten times Lord Mayor between 1930 and 1955.

Dubliner Ronnie Delany wins 1500 metres at Melbourne Olympics.

1957   Fianna Fáil returns to office at General Election, with Eamon de Valera back as Taoiseach.

Samuel Beckett's *Fin de partie* is performed for first time (again in London).

First Dublin Theatre Festival.

Alan Simpson, director of the Pike Theatre, is arrested for producing *The Rose Tattoo* by Tennessee Williams.

Gough Monument (Phoenix Park) blown up. The equestrian statue (by Foley) of the hero of the Peninsular War had been erected in 1880.

1958   Inauguration of Aer Lingus flights to North America.

An Foras Talúntais (Agricultural Research Institute) established.

British Association for the Advancement of Science meets in Dublin.

First public performance of Brendan Behan's *The Hostage* at the Halla Damer, St Stephen's Green.

1959   Eamon de Valera resigns as Taoiseach to become President of Ireland.

Seán Lemass becomes Taoiseach until 1966.

Harcourt Street railway station (and the line to Bray) is closed.

Inaugural conference in Dublin of Irish Congress of Trade Unions.